I0759221

# HORSE SENSE

## QUOTES ABOUT HORSES

Compiles by and Photos by Larry Stimeling

DEDICATED TO

THE SALT RIVER WILD HORSES

AND

WILD HORSES THROUGHOUT

THE UNITED STATES

AND THE FIGHT TO KEEP THEM

WILD AND FREE

# FORWARD

This book was made to create awareness for the fight to keep wild horses in the United States "Wild and Free". There are some who fail to see the importance and significance of the wild horses in America.

Throughout history the admiration of horses in general and wild horses in particular has been documented. The quotes here are a sampling of the words describing horses. They are not my own words.

The photographs were all taken in the month of July 2017 at Butcher Jones Recreational site in the Tonto National Forest near Mesa, Arizona. They were all taken by me with a Nicon coolpix B700 camera.

P;ease enjoy the photos and the quotes and join the fight to keep America's wild horses "WILD AND FREE"

# HORSE SENSE

## QUOTES ABOUT HORSES

Compiles by and Photos by Larry Stimeling

The essential joy of being with horses is that it brings us in contact with the rare elements of grace, beauty, spirit and fire.

Shannon Ralls Lemon

**Amazing horses Truest Majestic Beauty Running wild and free.**

**Jessie Host**

Horses and children, I often think, have a lot of the good sense there is in the world. ~

Josephine Demott Robinson

"A man that don't love a horse, there is something the matter with him." - Will Rogers

**Horses make a landscape look beautiful.**

*Alice Walker*

**The horse is a mirror to your soul and sometimes you**

**might not like what you see in the mirror.**

*Buck Brannaman*

A horse doesn't care how much you know until he

knows how much you care.

*Pat Parelli*

**The wildest colts make the best horses.**

*Plutarch*

**A horse is a thing of beauty... none will tire of looking**

**at him as long as he displays himself in his splendor.**

*Xenophon*

**The horse … beauty unsurpassed, strength**

**immeasurable and grace unlike any other,**

*Amber Senti*

**Whoever said a horse was dumb, was dumb.**

*Will Rogers*

**The horse is God's gift to mankind.**

*Arabian Proverb*

**There is something about the outside of a horse that is**

**good for the inside of a man.**

*Winston Churchill*

A pony is a childhood dream. A horse is an adulthood

treasure.

*Rebecca Carroll*

**Horses change lives.**

**Toni Robbinsson**

A horse is the projection of peoples' dreams about

themselves - strong, powerful, beautiful - and it has

the capability of giving us escape from our mundane

existence.

*Pam Brown*

**Man can learn a lot from wild horses … they are a
perfect example of  "It takes a village to raise a child."
Over heard on the Lower Salt River**

**Horses provide peace and tranquility to troubled**

**souls- they give us hope.**

**Toni Robinsos**

**A horse is worth more than riches.**

*Spanish Proverb*

**The earth would be nothing without the people, but man nothing without the horse."**

**~ Author Unknown.**

"I have seen things so beautiful they have brought tears to my eyes.
Yet none of them can match the gracefulness and beauty of a horse running free."

~ Author Unknown

No one can watch the wild horses for any length of
time and walk away without an inner peace.
Laurence Stimeling

"I've spent most of my life watching wild horses. The rest I've just wasted."

~ Author Unknown

"To many, the words love, hope and dreams are synonymous with wild horses."

~ Author Unknown

All horses deserve, at least once in their lives, to be loved by a little girl."

~ Author Unknown

Horse thou art truly a marvelous creature, for thou flys without wings and conquers without sword."

~ Author Unknown

"The love for a horse is just as complicated as the love for another human being...
if you never love a horse, you will never understand."

~ Author Unknown

**A dog may be man's best friend...but the horse wrote history."**

**~ Author Unknown**

**Bread may feed my body, but my horse feeds my soul."**

**~ Author Unknown**

"No philosophers so thoroughly comprehend us as dogs and horses."

~ Herman Melville

**We are so fortunate to be able to see the wild horses in their natural habitat**

**Johne Shelabarger**

**Wild horses hold a great economic, ecological, scientific as well as educational value.**

**Simone Netherlands**

"Ask me to show you poetry in motion and I will show you a horse."

~ Author Unknown

**A horse who bears himself proudly is a thing of such beauty and astonishment that he attracts the eyes of all beholders.**

**~ Xenophon.**

**"To see a horse is to see an angel on earth."**

**~ Author Unknown**

"Before I loved horses, I had nothing to live for. Now I love horses and can't stop seeing things to live for."

~ Author Unknown

The more things change, the more they stay the same. Itt is estimated that in the 1800s over 5 million buffalo roamed the great Plains of America.

By 1880 there were 5,000 hunters and tanners involved in the slaughter of wild buffalo. A single buffalo hide was worth up to $300. In an economy that was still recovering from the civil war.

At one point the Texas legislature was debating a bill that would protect the buffalo form hunters. General Phillip Sheridan addressed the Texas Legislature and said about the buffalo hunters,, "These men have done more in the last two years, and will do more in the next year, to settle the vexed Indian question, than the entire regular army has done in the last forty years. They are destroying the Indians' commissary.

And it is a well known fact that an army losing its base of supplies is placed at a great disadvantage. Send them powder and lead, if you will; but for a lasting peace, let them kill, skin, and sell until the buffaloes are exterminated. Then your prairies can be covered with speckled cattle.".

Since the slaughter to near extinction of the America Buffalo, much effort has been made to protect and grow the buffalo population.

Today we are talking about the U/S. Government sponsoring the slaughter of another American Icon in the west, the Wild Horses.

The Bureau  of Land Management (BLM) is poised to "kill, skin and sell" the wild horses until they are exterminated.  All of this for range land for cattle ranchers.

We, as horse advocates, cannot and must not allow this to happen. It is up to us to speak for the wild horses in America. . We must speak with a loud and united voice that says, " DO NOT SLAUGHTER THE ICONIC WILD HORSES IN AMERICA!"


How can you help?

* letters to your Representative in Congress and to your Senators  Dmeanding protection for  ALL WILD HORSES AND BURROS in the United States.

*Follow this up with Phone calls and Emails to their Local and DC offices.

* If possible schedule a face to face meeting with them.

# Do't Delay ... DO IT TODAY

## THE HORSES OF BUTCHER JONES RECREATION SITE

Photographs of the Salt River Wild Horses that frequently visited the Butcher Jones Recreation Site in the Tonto National Forest near Mesa, Arizona.A portion of the proceeds will be donated to the Salt River Wild Horse Management Group a 501(c)3 nonprofit organization dedicated to protecting the Salt River...

List Price: $30.00

**DIAMOND FREE AND WILD** Photo-biography of Diamond, one of the Salt River Wild Horses.

List Price: $20.00

## HORSE SENSE

A compilation of Quotes about horses especially wild horses. These sayings are paired photographs of the iconic wild horses ehat make the area along the lower Salt River near Mesa Arizona their home.
List Price: $15.

## BLOOMING ARIZONA

Photographs of the beautiful flowers growing in Arizona.

List Price $20

## THERE'S SNOW ON THE MOUNTAIN

Larry Stimeling takes you to see the beauty of thedesert mountain when it is covered with snow.

List Price: $10.00

**FROM THE WALL SECOND EDITION**
A compilation of information and stories about some of the men and women whose names are on the Vietnam Veterans Memorial. The information was gathered from several data bases. The stories are personal accounts of incidents that happened during his visits to displays of the replicas of The Wall.
List Price: $20.00

**FROM ARIZONA TO THE WALL**
A companion book to From The Wall, From Arizona to the Wall is a compilation of information about those who died in the Vietnam War, Those who never returned (MIAs) and those who died later from Agent Orange exposure or PTSD related suicide. Included in the book are interesting facts about the Vietnam...

List Price: $12.50

**ON'T TELL ME WE LOST**
**A Vietnam Veteran's perspective on the perceived outcome of the war and the things that influenced that perceived outcome.**
**Publication Date: December 24, 2015**
**List Price: $10.00**